11 Plus
Maths
Assessment Papers

CONTENTS

Introduction

This book contains 10 maths papers to prepare for the 11+. Eleven plus examinations are administered by the examination boards GL assessment and CEM assessment. While both broadly cover the same eleven plus topics, the examination itself is very different depending on whether a particular school favours GL assessment or the CEM. Irrespective of which board you are preparing for, these papers will be a useful addition to a program of study.

The papers can be used as examination practise papers. Allow 40 minutes to complete the tests. Alternatively, the papers can be used as a learning activity to improve familiarity with the style of questions typical on eleven plus and entrance examinations.

Each paper consists of a variety of questions worth 35 marks.

There is a self-assessment section for students to reflect on their next steps and to record their scores. A particular score on these papers cannot guarantee success in eleven plus as this often depends on the scores of other candidates on the day of the test.

Information for students - How to use this book

- If you are using the papers as tests, it's important to take the time after the test to check your answers and to discuss the correct answers with the adult who helps you.

- There may be a few words used in questions that you haven't met before. You should use a dictionary at the end of the test to check these words to expand your own vocabulary.

- If you have time at the end of the test, check your answers to see if you made any mistakes.

- In a test situation with a set time, try to give answers to all of the questions. At the end of the test, you should tell the adult who helps you if you were unsure of any answers so that together you can discuss the correct answer.

Self-assessment

You may find it useful to record your scores for each paper and to reflect on how you can improve. You may find that you need to:

- practise your times tables
- ensure you have understood the requirements of a question
- answer all parts of a question
- revise how to answer certain types of question
- remember to check answers if there is time

Paper 1   Score out of 35 [   ]   Percentage [   ]

Things I can do to improve.

[   ]

Paper 2   Score out of 35 [   ]   Percentage [   ]

Things I can do to improve.

[   ]

Paper 3   Score out of 35 [   ]   Percentage [   ]

Things I can do to improve.

[   ]

Paper 4   Score out of 35 [   ]   Percentage [   ]

Things I can do to improve.

[   ]

Paper 5   Score out of 35 [   ]   Percentage [   ]

Things I can do to improve.

[   ]

Paper 6   Score out of 35 [   ]   Percentage [   ]

Things I can do to improve.

[   ]

Paper 7   Score out of 35 [   ]   Percentage [   ]

Things I can do to improve.

[   ]

Paper 8   Score out of 35 [   ]   Percentage [   ]

Things I can do to improve.

[   ]

Paper 9   Score out of 35 [   ]   Percentage [   ]

Things I can do to improve.

[   ]

Paper 10   Score out of 35 [   ]   Percentage [   ]

Things I can do to improve.

[   ]

Progress Chart

If you wish, you can shade in or colour the bars to plot your progress.

Don't worry if your score goes down sometimes. Every time you complete a test and look at the mark scheme, you will be learning and improving your skills.

You can calculate the percentage by multiplying your score by 100 then dividing by 35.

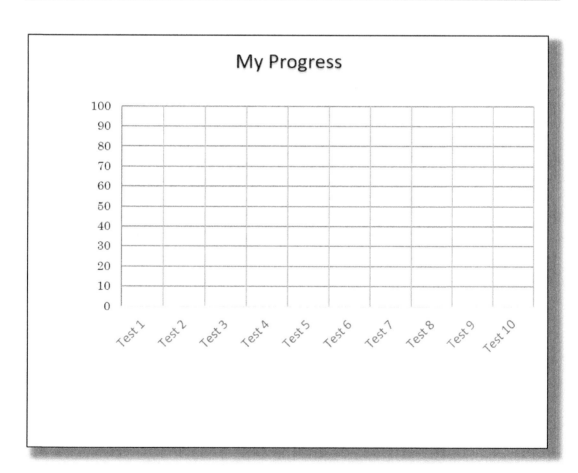

Useful Information

Names of 3D Shapes

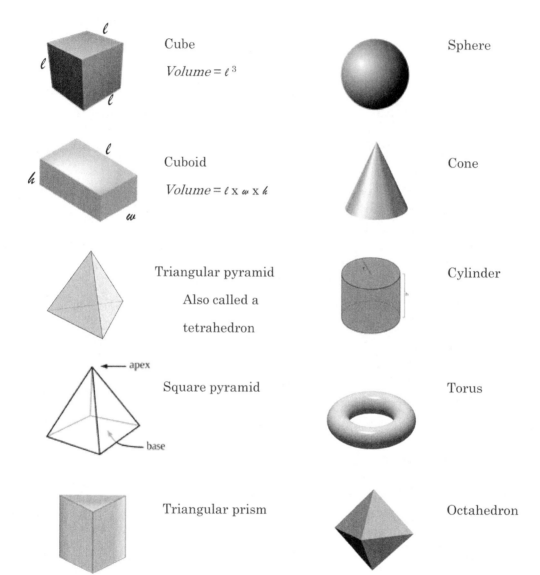

Cube

$Volume = \ell^3$

Sphere

Cuboid

$Volume = \ell \times w \times h$

Cone

Triangular pyramid

Also called a

tetrahedron

Cylinder

apex

Square pyramid

Torus

base

Triangular prism

Octahedron

Polygons

Polygons are closed figures or shapes with straight sides.

A **scalene triangle** is a triangle where all sides are different lengths.

A **quadrilateral** has four sides. The shapes to the right are all quadrilaterals.

1	**Parallelogram**	2	**Rectangle**
3	**Rhombus**	4	**Trapezoid**

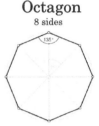

(You'll know what a square looks like)

Pentagon	**Hexagon**	**Heptagon**	**Octagon**
5 sides	6 sides	7 sides	8 sides

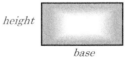
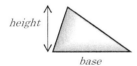

Areas of 2D Shapes

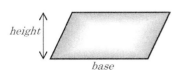

Square Area = Base x Height

Rectangle Area = Base x Height

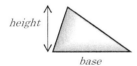

Triangle Area = (Base x Height) ÷ 2

Trapezoid Area = [(a+b) x h] ÷ 2

Parallelogram Area =
Base x Perpendicular Height

Rhombus Area = (Length x Height) ÷ 2

Save Some Time

You don't have to remember these methods, but if you can remember some, it could gain you time in a test.

Multiplying by 5 for an even number
Example: 5 x 18

Divide the number by 2. $\dfrac{18}{2} = 9$

Add a zero at the end. .   **90**

Multiplying by 5 for an odd number
Example: 5 x 19

Take one away from the number $19 - 1 = 18$

Divide the result by 2. $\dfrac{18}{2} = 9$

Add a five at the end.   **95**

Calculating 5 percent of a number
Example: 5% of 464

Shift the decimal point one place to the left   46.4

Divide this by 2.   **23.2**

(*You can find 15% by finding 5% and multiplying by 3 etc.*)

Square a two-digit number ending in 5
Example: 45^2

Multiply the first digit by (itself + 1) $4 \times (4+1) = 20$

Put 25 after this number.   **2025**

Subtract a large number from 1000
Example: $1000 - 583$

Subtract all except for the final number from 9, then subtract the final number from 10.

$9 - 5 = 4$ $9 - 8 = 1$ $10 - 3 = 7$ **417**

Will it divide?

A number is ...

Divisible by 2 if the last digit is a multiple of 2 (or is 0). So, 178 works because 8 is divisible by 2.

$^{178}/_2 = \textbf{89}$

Divisible by 3 if the sum of the digits is divisible by 3. So, 738 works because the digits (7 + 3 + 8), add up to 18 which is divisible by 3.

$^{738}/_3 = \textbf{144}$

Divisible by 4 if the last two digits are divisible by 4. So, 7344 works because 44 is divisible by 4.

$^{7344}/_4 = \textbf{1836}$

Divisible by 5 if the last digit is 0 or 5. So, 7725 works.

$^{7725}/_5 = \textbf{1545}$

Divisible by 6 if it passes the rules for both 2 and 3. So, 426 works. 6 is a multiple of 2 and 4 + 2 + 6 = 12 which is divisible by 3.

$^{426}/_6 = \textbf{71}$

Divisible by 9 if the sum of the digits is divisible by 9. So, 6381 works since 6 + 3 + 8 + 1 = 18, which is divisible by 9.

$^{6381}/_9 = \textbf{709}$

Divisible by 10 if the number ends in a 0.

$^{8910}/_{10} = \textbf{891}$

Paper One

1) What is 215% of 80?

.... (1)

2) What is 0.74 x 0.05?

.... (1)

3) What is $3x - 4y$ when $x = 7$ and $y = -2$?

.... (1)

4) What is the square root of 169?

.... (1)

5) A cube has a volume of 8cm^3. Another box has edges which are twice as long. What is the volume of the larger cube in cm^3?

.... (2)

6) Write down any fraction between a quarter and a half.

.... (1)

7) If 750g of pasta costs £1.02 how much is a kilogram of pasta?

.... (1)

8) What is the difference between 10% of 18 and 20% of 29.6?

.... **(2)**

9) I turn 30 degrees clockwise, 80 degrees anticlockwise and finally 90 degrees clockwise. If I want to return to my original position by turning through the smallest angle possible, in which direction should I turn and what should the angle be?

.... **(2)**

10) Saskia has two brothers, Joe and Sam. She shares out her grapes. She gives Joe twice as many as she gives herself and she gives Sam half as many as she gives herself. If there are 91 grapes in total, how many does Saskia get?

.... **(2)**

11) Put these numbers in order of size.

0.46 $^3/_7$ 43.7% $^9/_{16}$

smallest .... largest **(1)**

14

12) Amar and Abi have saved a total of £458 for their holiday. Abi saved £72 more than Amar. How much did Abi save?

.... (2)

13) Expand and simplify $3(y - 2) - 5(2y - 1)$

.... (2)

14) What is $^{12}/_3 \div ^3/_4$?

.... (1)

15) On a farm, 6 out of every 25 acres of the land are used to grow crops. Wheat is grown on $^5/_8$ of the land used to grow crops. What percentage of the total area of the land on the farm is used to grow wheat?

.... (2)

16) Here are two identical squares. The first one is divided into quarters and the second is divided into fifths. What fraction of the whole shape is shaded?

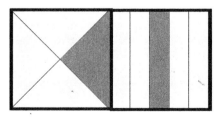

.... (2)

17) A rectangle has a length of x + 4 cm and a width of 2x − 7 cm. If the perimeter is 42cm, what is the value of x?

.... (2)

18) A volcano erupts and produces a cloud of hot gas of temperature 800 degrees Celsius. When this cloud reached the nearest town, it had cooled to a temperature of 520 degrees Celsius. What was the percentage decrease in temperature of the gas cloud?

.... (2)

19) The length and width of the swimming pool is 5m by 3m. The 1m wide path will be tiled with 50x50cm tiles. The tiles are sold in boxes of 15. How many boxes are needed to cover the path?

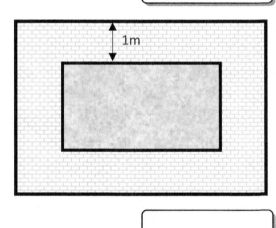

.... (2)

20) The difference between a quarter of a certain number and one fifth of the number, is 7. What is the number?

.... (2)

16

21) A chocolate bar is shared between Susie and Arnav in the ratio 5:1. If Susie has 80g more than Arnav, what was the original weight of the chocolate bar?

.... (2)

22) What is the volume of a box which is 12.5 cm by 6.5cm by 7 cm?

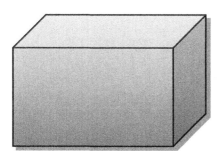

.... (1)

End of paper 1

Paper Two

1) What is the product of 7 and 6 divided by the sum of 9 and 5?

.... (1)

2) What is $2^3/_4$ x $^{35}/_6$?

.... (2)

3) a) Here is a number machine for the expression 4w - 8

w → [x 4] → [-8] →

Draw a number machine for the following expression:

5y + 7

.... (2)

b) calculate the output if the value of y is 13

.... (1)

4) Find 0.65 of 260

.... (1)

5) If it is −26.5°C in Scotland and 34.5°C in Australia, what is the difference in temperature?

.... (1)

6) Complete the magic square. Each row, column and diagonal have to add up to the same number.

-4		0
	-1	
-2		2

(4)

7) The mean height of 7 girls is 154cm. If another girl joins the class who is 150cm tall, what is the new mean height of the group of girls?

.... **(2)**

8) Which is best value?

Asdi, Sunsburys and Mortisons sells chocolate mini eggs at the following prices. Which is the best value shop for mini eggs?

Asdi	1 kg for £5.90
Sunsburys	100g for 80p
Mortisons	250g for £1.20

.... **(2)**

9) If six Pounds are worth seven Euros, and two Euros are worth three Australian Dollars. How many Australian Dollars are four Pounds worth?

10) A rare postage stamp was bought for £300 in 1980. Its value at that time was just 12% of its current value. Calculate the current value of the stamp.

.... (1)

11) While taking part in a 10 km race, a runner completed the first 6500 m in 26 minutes.

a) Calculate the average speed of the runner, in km per hour, over this section of the course.

.... (2)

b) The runner completed the remaining 3500m in 24 mins. What was his average speed during the race?

.... (2)

12) Every athlete in a team drinks 3.6 litres of water each day. The whole team drinks 18 litres in a day. How many athletes are there in the team?

.... (1)

13) A bag of raisins is shared between Jemma and Tyler in the ratio 11:5. If Jemma has 60 more raisins than Tyler, how many raisins did they have to share in total?

.... (2)

14) The wage bill for five builders and six carpenters is £1,340, while the bill for eight builders and three carpenters is £1,220. What wage is paid to each builder?

.... (2)

15) Marcus has a bag of counters numbered 1 – 150. What is the probability of taking...

a) a square number?

.... (1)

b) a cube number?

.... (1)

c) a multiple of 7?

7/14, 28,28 35 42

.... (1)

16) A bag of 40 discs contains a mixture of red and blue discs. If the probability of taking a blue is 0.35, how many are blue and how many are red?

0.65

.... (2)

17) The pie chart shows the percentages of different coloured flowers in a garden.

There are 40 pink flowers. How many red flowers are there?

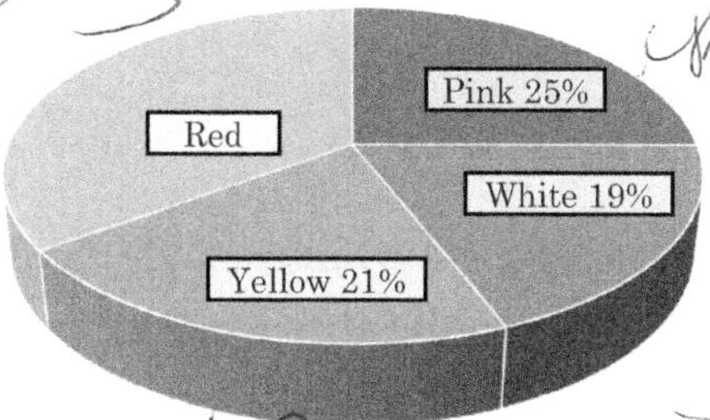

Pink 25%

Red

White 19%

Yellow 21%

35

.... (2)

End of paper 2

Paper Three

1) Work out 789.3 + 24.05

.... (1)

2) Divide 840 by 20

.... (1)

3) Multiply 4.5 by 3.9

.... (1)

4) Express $\dfrac{19}{25}$ as a decimal

.... (1)

5) Work out 3.45 + 11.01 + 2.3

.... (1)

6) A farmer arranges 78247 cabbages into 169 crates. How many cabbages are in each crate?

.... (1)

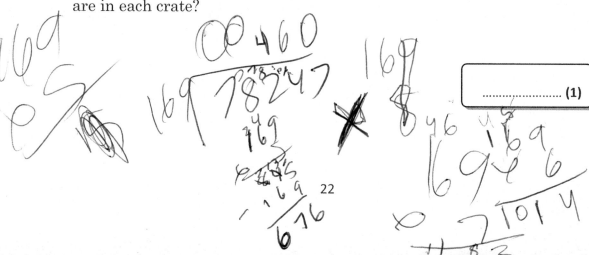

22

7) Football supporters are being transported from a stadium by coach. Each coach can hold 80 supporters.

a) How many coaches are needed to transport 1975 supporters?

.... (2)

b) If all of the coaches are completely filled with supporters apart from the last coach, how many people are in the last coach?

.... (1)

8) What is the smallest angle between the hands on a clock at the following times?

a) 2pm

.... (1)

b) 5pm

.... (1)

c) 2.30pm

.... (1)

d) 3.30pm

.... (1)

9) Find the value of y

a) $5y - 8 = 47$

.... (1)

b) $7y + 4 = 25$

.... (1)

10) The length of a rectangle is four times bigger than the width. If the area is 144cm² what is the perimeter?

.... **(2)**

11) A plumber uses the following equation to charge clients for a call out.

$$C = 10 + 12h + \text{cost of the parts}$$

C is the cost in £ and h is the number of hours the job takes.

Calculate the following:

a) How much does the plumber charge for every hour she works?

.... **(1)**

b) A job that takes 3 hours and involves fitting a shower at a cost of £257

.... **(2)**

c) A job that takes 2 hours 45 mins and involves fitting a new tap at cost of £82.50

.... **(2)**

d) If a job cost £138 and the parts cost £80, for how many hours did the plumber work on the job?

.... **(2)**

12) The average number of penalty corners awarded to Chelmsford Hockey Team over their last 5 matches was 8.2

If they received a total of 34 penalty corners in 4 of these matches, how many were awarded in the fifth match?

.... (2)

13) a) Shereen spent 38% of her money on the first day of her holiday. What <u>fraction</u> of her money did she have left?

.... (1)

b) If she spent £57 on her first day, how much money did she have to start with?

.... (2)

14) a) Carl was absent from school for $\dfrac{1}{25}$ of the Spring term. What percentage of the Spring term was he absent for?

.... (1)

b) If the Spring term consisted of 125 days, for how many days was Carl absent?

.... (1)

15) Purple paint is made by mixing blue and red paint in the ratio 5:3. How many litres of blue paint do I need to make 32 litres of purple paint?

4

.... (2)

16) A house costs £200,000 in 2020 and in 2021 its price has increased to £220,000. What is the percentage increase in price?

20,000

.... (2)

End of paper 3

Paper Four

1) Work out 6701 – 125

.... (1)

2) Multiply 49 by 7

.... (1)

3) Divide 9608 by 8

.... (1)

4) Add the sum of 4 and 7 to the product of 6 and 9.

.... (1)

5) Work out $^3/_8 + ^1/_6$

.... (1)

6) Work out $^1/_4 - ^5/_9$

.... (1)

7) Find 15% of 260

.... (1)

27

8) Three friends share a birthday pizza. Ryan has a fifth of the pizza and Katie has three eighths. What fraction of the pizza is left for Louisa?

.... (2)

9) Add together 15mm, 65cm and 1.04m

.... (1)

10) a) This cube has faces each with an area of 64cm² What is the surface area of the cube?

.... (1)

b) What is the total length of all the edges?

.... (1)

c) If the cube is cut in half along the line in the middle and separated into two cuboids, what is the combined surface area of the two new cuboids?

.... (1)

11) Omar went shopping and bought 3 computer games that cost £25.50 each and 2 memory sticks that cost £4.30 each. How much change did Omar get from £100?

.... (2)

12) A coffee and 3 crème eggs cost £2.25. Three coffees and 3 crème egg costs £4.65. What is the cost of a coffee and what is the cost of a crème egg?

coffee .... crème egg .... (2)

13) What is a fifth of a quarter of 500?

.... (2)

14) Kim lends David £8. David pays back 20.5% the next day. How much does he still owe?

.... (2)

15) Thomas spent £42 on DVD's. Some cost £5 and some cost £9. Thomas bought the same number of each DVD. How many of each type of DVD did Thomas buy?

.... (2)

29

16) Esha ran 4 km in 14 minutes. Jackie started 90 seconds later and finished 30 seconds sooner. What was Jackie's speed in km per hour?

.... (2)

17) This is part of the timetable for Anglian railways trains from Liverpool Street to Colchester. Chelmsford is exactly half way in terms of time between Hatfield Peverel and Witham.

London Liverpool Street	11.30
Stratford	12.16
Shenfield	12.44
Hatfield Peverel	13.10
Chelmsford	
Witham	14.06
Colchester	14.44

a) How long in minutes does it take to travel from Stratford to Hatfield Peverel?

.... (1)

b) How long in mins does it take to travel from Shenfield to Chelmsford?

.... (1)

c) A return train travelling in the opposite direction at the same speed leaves Colchester at ten to nine in the evening. What will the timetable show as its arrival time in Witham?

.... (1)

d) When will the return train reach London Liverpool Street?

.... (1)

30

18) Marco has seven Shetland ponies. They have a mean height of 116cm. Marco buys an eighth pony. The height of this pony is 128cm.

Find the mean height of all eight ponies.

.... (2)

19) The mean height of seven pupils is 123cm. One pupil of height 147cm leaves the group. Find the mean height of the remaining six pupils.

.... (2)

20) $\frac{1}{4}$ of the stock on a deli counter is cheeses, $\frac{1}{3}$ are sausages, $\frac{1}{6}$ is salami and the rest are bread rolls. If there are 720 items in the shop, how many bread rolls are there?

End of paper 4

.... (2)

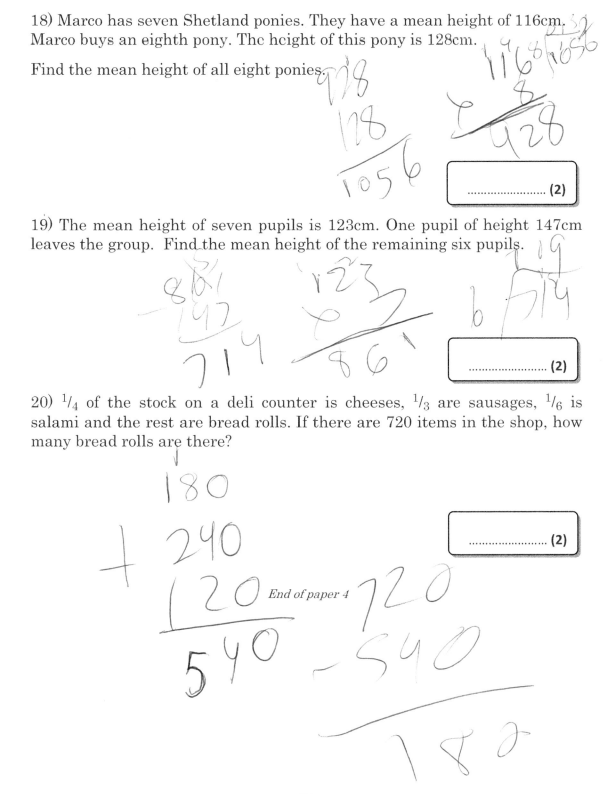

Paper Five

1) What is $9.76 - {}^3/_5$? (give your answer as a decimal)

9 .1 0
0 . 6

.... (1)

2) What is a fifth of 400,000?

4

.... (1)

3) Joanna chooses a number. She divides her number by 7 and gets a remainder of 3. Name 3 possible numbers that Joanna might have chosen.

.... (1)

4) What is 26 divided by 0.5?

.... (1)

5) What is 125% of 380?

.... (1)

6) There are 12 students in Mr Thompson's Maths group. The mean mark in a test is 76%. In Mr Smith's group there are only 8 students. Their mean mark is 84%.

Find the overall mean for the 20 children.

.... (2)

7) a) A sequence has the formula 3n + 7. Write the first 2 terms for this sequence.

.... & .... **(2)**

b) What is the 50th term for this sequence?

.... **(1)**

8) The ratio of boys to girls in a school is 3:4. If there are 854 children in the school, how many are boys and how many are girls?

122
× 3
366

122
× 4
488

...........boys & ....girls **(2)**

9) A grocery store buys 6 boxes of pears for £5 a box. Each box contains 90 pears. The store discards 10% of the pears as they are rotten. If the store sells pears for 15p each how much profit can they make selling the remaining pears?

30

.... **(2)**

10) Nina needs to be in the Paris office by 3pm for a meeting. Her flight takes off from Gatwick airport at 7.50am. It takes 40 mins to get to the airport from her house. She expects to spend 2 hours checking in her luggage and going through airport security at Gatwick. The flight time is 2hrs 15 mins. Paris is 2 hours ahead of the time at Gatwick. When she lands, she expects that it will take one hour to go through passport control and collect her luggage. There is then a 30minute taxi ride to the office.

a) What is the latest time she should leave her house to catch the flight to Paris from Gatwick?

.... **(2)**

b) At what time will the flight land in local time?

.... **(1)**

c) At what time will she arrive at the meeting?

.... **(1)**

11) This is a sector cut from a circle with an area of 270cm^2. The angle of this sector is 40°.

What is the area of this sector?

.... **(2)**

12) A scalene triangle has one angle which is 73.7 degrees and another angle which is 24.5 degrees. How big is the third angle?

.... **(1)**

13) Students are put into 9 classes. 5 classes each have 29 students. The other 4 groups have an equal number of students. Altogether there are 205 students. How many students are there in each of the other 4 groups?

.... **(2)**

34

14) Craig has ten coins. He has only 10p, 20p and 50p coins (at least one of each). The ten coins total £3.20 Work out how many of each coin he has.

> .... x 10p   .... x 20p   .... x 50p **(1)**

15) Three bags each contain the same number of discs. 2 discs are taken out of one of the bags. There are now 5 discs in this bag. Work out the total number of discs that are now in the three bags.

> .... **(1)**

16) Bottles of squash cost 89p each. Phoebe pays for 39 bottles of squash with a £50 note. How much change should she get?

> .... **(1)**

17) A supermarket sells cans of tuna in the following sizes. Which is the best value?

250g = £0.90   750g = £3.00   400g = £1.80

> .... g **(2)**

18) a) Write a formula for the nth term of this sequence.

15   9   3   -3

.... **(2)**

b) Calculate the 10th 25th and 80th term.

10th .... 25th .... 80th .... **(3)**

19) Name the following 3D shapes from the net of the shape:

a)

.... **(1)**

b)

.... **(1)**

End of paper 5

Paper Six

1) What is the sum of 5.4kg and 365g?

.... (1)

2) Add 0.78 and $^3/_4$. Write your answer as a decimal.

.... (1)

3) A number is divided by 7 and the answer is 25. What is the number?

.... (1)

4) Multiply 4.35 by 2.4

.... (1)

5) How many ml are there in 6.57 litres?

.... (1)

6) Work out $-18 \div -3$

.... (1)

7) Mr Green goes into a café and buys one pack of sandwiches, one packet of biscuits and two cups of tea and is charged £3.15. Mrs Plum goes into the café and buys a pack of sandwiches and one packet of biscuits and is charged £2.25.

a) How much would it cost for one pack of sandwiches, one packet of biscuits and one cup of tea?

.... (1)

37

b) If a packet of biscuits is 75p and sandwiches are £1.50. How much change would you get from a £20 note if you bought 2 sandwiches, 3 packets of biscuits and a tea?

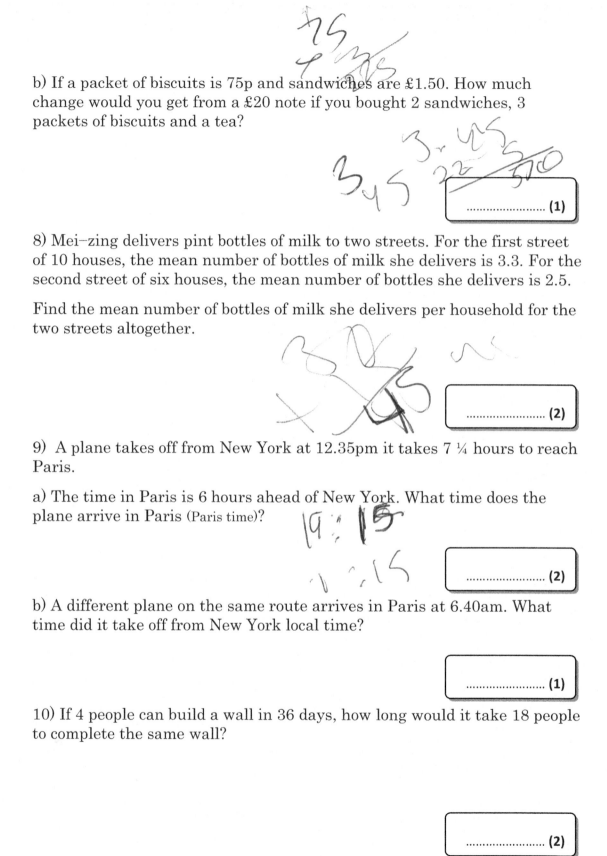

.... (1)

8) Mei–zing delivers pint bottles of milk to two streets. For the first street of 10 houses, the mean number of bottles of milk she delivers is 3.3. For the second street of six houses, the mean number of bottles she delivers is 2.5.

Find the mean number of bottles of milk she delivers per household for the two streets altogether.

.... (2)

9) A plane takes off from New York at 12.35pm it takes 7 ¼ hours to reach Paris.

a) The time in Paris is 6 hours ahead of New York. What time does the plane arrive in Paris (Paris time)?

.... (2)

b) A different plane on the same route arrives in Paris at 6.40am. What time did it take off from New York local time?

.... (1)

10) If 4 people can build a wall in 36 days, how long would it take 18 people to complete the same wall?

.... (2)

11) A square has a perimeter of 48cm. What is the area of the square?

.... (1)

12) A rectangle has perimeter 96cm. The rectangle is five times as long as it is wide. What is the area of the rectangle?

.... (2)

13) The floor or a room is 3 metres wide and 4 metres long. I am going to tile the floor with tiles that are 50 centimetres wide and 50 centimetres long. How many tiles do I need to buy?

2500   7000

.... (2)

14) Residents are being evacuated from an island by boat. Each boat can hold 106 residents.

a) How many boats are needed to transport 20040 residents?

.... (2)

b) If all of the boats are completely filled with residents apart from the last boat, how many people are in the last boat?

.... (1)

15) A garage stocks several makes of car.

      200 Audis   60 Porche   100 BMW   160 Mazda   80 Vauxhall

a) How many cars are there?

160

360   16

.... (1)

b) How many degrees on a pie chart would the sector be for

i) Audi

.... (1)

ii) Porche

.... (1)

iii) BMW

.... (1)

iv) Mazda

.... (1)

v) Vauxhall

.... (1)

16) There are 35 packets of crisps in a box. Joan buys 5 boxes. She buys each box for £2.99. She sells the packets for 40p each. How much money does she make?

.... (2)

17) Otto's age is a square number. Harry's age is a cube number. Harry is 2 years older than Otto. How old are Otto and Harry?

.... (2)

18) These are the ages of players in a basketball team:

Name	Adam	Karen	Colin	Kevin	Florence
Age	18	25	26	24	17

a) What is the median?

.... (1)

b) What is the range?

.... (1)

End of paper 6

Paper Seven

1) What is 200 divided by 0.4?

.... **(1)**

2) How many nines are there in fifty-four?

.... **(1)**

3) What number should you add to negative three to get the answer five?

.... **(1)**

4) Add two point five to three quarters.

.... **(1)**

5) What is a quarter of an eighth of 96?

.... **(1)**

6) What is 100 divided by negative 5?

.... **(1)**

7) Use greater than or less than symbols in the gaps below

$^5/_6$ .... 0.4 $^3/_7$ 65%

37mm .... 3cm   6.4m 100cm

$^{27}/_{45}$ .... 38% $^{14}/_{42}$ 0.35

(6)

8) I think of a number. When I multiply this number by 15 and then subtract 7, I get 38.

What number am I thinking of?

.... (1)

9) Kanye, Josie and Sarah share a bag of sweets. Kanye gets 5 more sweets than Josie, and Sarah gets twice as many sweets as Kanye. Sarah gets 22 sweets. How many sweets are there in the bag?

.... (2)

10) I have a rectangular piece of paper with sides of 18cm and 5.5cm. If I fold the paper in half along the short side, what is the new area of the paper?

.... (1)

11) If $x = 5$, $y = -3$ and $z = 7$ find the value of

   a) xyz

   .... (1)

   b) $2y^2z$

   .... (1)

   c) $2x^2y$

   .... (1)

   d) $x^2 + y$

   .... (1)

   e) $5(y - z)^2$

   .... (1)

   f) xy^2

   .... (1)

12) A bat flies at an average speed of thirty kilometres per hour. At this speed, how far would it fly in...

a) one minute

$$60 \overline{\smash{)}30{.}000}$$

.... (1)

b) 45 minutes

.... (1)

c) 0.4 of an hour?

.... (1)

13) The difference between a fifth of a certain number and one quarter of the number is 5. What is the number?

.... (2)

14) Work out the value of x if $\dfrac{3}{8} + \dfrac{1}{8} = \dfrac{1}{x}$

.... (2)

15) Find angle A

.... (2)

16) The sum of two numbers is 100. The different between them is 56. What is the larger number?

.... (2)

17) $\frac{1}{9}$ of the shirts sold in a sports shop are Chelsea shirts. $\frac{5}{8}$ of the remainder are Leeds UTD. The rest of the shirts are Aston Villa. If the shop has 63 Aston Villa shirts, how many more Chelsea shirts are there than Aston Villa?

.... (2)

End of paper 7

Paper Eight

1) What is 0.35 of 200?

.... (1)

2) What is 87% of 400?

.... (1)

3) Calculate 9 + 4 x 7

.... (1)

4) Divide 463 by 5. Write your answer as a decimal.

.... (1)

5) Multiply 4.3 by 3.8

.... (1)

6) Write four hundred and ten thousand five hundred and nine in figures.

.... (1)

7) I think of a number. I square my number and add 7. My answer is 71. What is my number?

.... (1)

8) If you are facing South, what is the smaller angle you have to turn through to face North-West?

.... (1)

9) How many minutes are there in 0.6 hours?

.... (1)

10)

a) Calculate the area of the larger rectangle on the right.

.... (1)

b) Calculate the total shaded area that the rectangles cover.

.... (2)

11) Find angle α

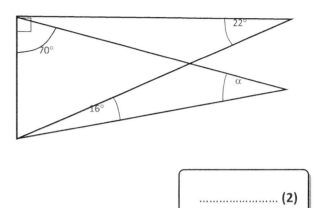

.... **(2)**

12) There are 624 pupils in a school. The ratio of boys to girls in this school is 7:6. How many girls and how many boys are in this school?

boys .... girls .... **(2)**

13) Joey has six blocks of wood and their total weight is 5kg. Five blocks weigh 850g each. What is the weight of the last block?

.... **(2)**

14) 64 pens cost £5.76. How much would 80 pens cost?

.... **(1)**

15) A computer costs £1960. It is then sold on for £1568. What is the percentage decrease in price?

.... **(2)**

16) There are physiotherapists and paediatricians at a meeting. There are 35 paediatricians. 30% of the people at the meeting are physiotherapists. How many people are at the meeting?

.... (2)

17) a) Write a formula for the nth term of this sequence

−9   −5   −1   3   7

.... (2)

b) Calculate the 12th 25th and 103rd term.

12th .... 25th .... 103rd .... (3)

18) Mika faces East. He turns 135° clockwise. How many degrees clockwise does he need to turn face North?

.... (1)

19) A delicatessen specialises in sausages. It displays 60 chorizo sausages; 24 Lincolnshire; 36 garlic sausages; 30 salami sausages; 50 pepperoni sausages and 40 sage sausages.

a) What fraction of the sausages are

i) chorizo?

.... (1)

ii) pepperoni?

.... (1)

b) If the owner displayed there produce on a pie chart, how many degrees would represent

i) Lincolnshire?

.... (1)

ii) pepperoni?

.... (1)

c) If a local restauranteur bought all the chorizo, calculate the fraction of the remaining sausages which are

i) salami

.... (1)

ii) pepperoni

.... (1)

End of paper 8

Paper Nine

1) Add together 0.3, 0.03, 3 and 0.003.

.... (1)

2) What is 0.789 x1000 ?

.... (1)

3) What is $\dfrac{0.63}{0.09}$?

.... (1)

4) What is 1.456km in cm ?

.... (1)

5) How many seconds are there in 2 hours?

.... (1)

6) A bucket holds 20 litres of water. 17 litres and 250 ml of it was taken out and then 3 litres and 780 ml was poured in it. How many litres of water is there in the bucket now?

.... (1)

7) 40 Farmers in Suffolk were interviewed about the numbers of livestock they keep. 24 said they kept sheep, 19 said they kept cows and 3 said they kept none of these animals.

Complete the Venn diagram using this information.

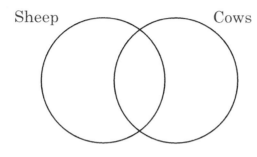

Sheep   Cows

(4)

8) Which container is made to hold approximately 2 litres?

bucket   bath
kettle   tea cup
teaspoon   tablespoon

.... (1)

9) Bryony will be x years old in 4 years. How old was she 6 years ago?

.... (2)

10) A map has a scale of 2cm to 5km. The distance between London and Dover is 62.5 km. What is the distance on the map between London and Dover?

.... (1)

11) What is 234% of 150?

12) The average number of goals scored by West Ham in the last five games was 6.4. If they got 27 goals in four of the matches, how many goals did they get in the fifth match?

13) A lottery win is divided in the ratio 4:9 amongst two people. If the smaller share is £78 what is the larger share?

14) The shaded corner squares (1cm x 1cm) are cut out of the 14cm by 8cm rectangle and the remaining shape folded to make a shallow open box. What is the capacity of the box in cm^3?

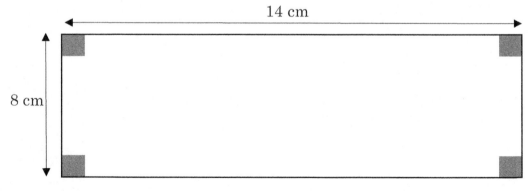

14 cm

8 cm

15) What is this number to two decimal places?

67.78934

.... **(1)**

16) Kylie saw a dress on sale for 25% off the original price plus another 10% off the discounted price. If the dress originally cost £88, how much did Kylie pay for the dress?

.... **(2)**

17) Calculate the area of rectangle in m² which is 70cm by 35cm long.

.... **(1)**

18) a) Express $6\frac{1}{4}$ as an improper fraction.

.... **(1)**

b) Now work out the square root of this improper fraction.

.... **(2)**

19) Sam runs around her athletics track. After running some laps, she has done one fifth of her target. After another two laps she has done a quarter of her target. What is her target number of laps?

.... **(2)**

20) Write 0.225 as a fraction in its lowest terms.

.... (2)

21) Two boxes inside a larger box both have seven boxes inside them. How many boxes are there in total?

.... (2)

22) What is $^7/_9$ divided by $^{12}/_5$?

.... (2)

End of paper 9

Paper Ten

1) Max has more than 5 apples but fewer than 9 apples. Paolo has more than 7 apples but fewer than 10 apples.

How many apples do Max and Paolo have altogether? List all the possibilities.

.... & .... & .... & .... **(1)**

2) What is a quarter of a fifth of 150?

.... **(1)**

3)   82 x 107= 8774

Use this to work out the following

a)   8774 ÷ 82

.... **(1)**

b)   8774 ÷ 107

.... **(1)**

c)   8774 ÷ 820

.... **(1)**

d)   820 x 1070

.... **(1)**

e)   82 x 1.07

.... **(1)**

4) Draw number machines for the following expressions.

a) $4x^2$

.... (2)

b) $12(x + 11)$

.... (2)

5) Use greater than or less than symbols in the gaps below.

$\dfrac{2}{3}$ .... 60%   0.801 .... 0.810   (4)

9^2 .... 9 x 2 5^3 127

6) It takes 5 machines 6 hours to produce 1000 DVDs. Work out how long it would take 4 machines to produce 1000 DVDs.

.... (2)

7) Favourite types of movie:

Complete the table below showing the number of people who prefer each type of movie and the pie chart angle.

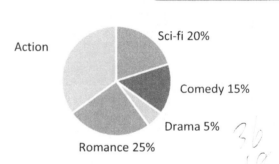

Action

Sci-fi 20%

Comedy 15%

Drama 5%

Romance 25%

Type of movie	Number	Size of angle on pie chart
Sci–fi		
Comedy		
Drama	12	18°
Romance		
Action		

(4)

56

8) A path in the school grounds is 3 metres wide and rectangular in shape. How long is the path if it covers an area of 48 square metres?

3m

.... (1)

9) Which of these number is closest to zero?

-0.4 0.2 0.005 -0.00006

.... (1)

10) If the digit 5 is replaced by the digit 6 in each of the numbers below, which number is increased by the largest amount?

7567   2385   561   253691

.... (1)

11) There are 30 beads in a bag. 5 are blue, 6 are yellow, 3 are red and the rest are orange.

a) What is the probability of picking an orange bead out of the bag?

.... (1)

b) What is the probability of picking a blue bead out of the bag?

.... (1)

c) What is the probability of picking either a yellow or red bead out of the bag?

.... (1)

12) A prize of £132 is divided in the ratio 5:7. What is the difference between the two shares?

.... (2)

13) The average number of goals scored by Plymouth in the last five games was 3.4. If they got 13 goals in four of the matches, how many goals did they get in the fifth match?

.... (2)

14) Work out the value of

a)   9 + 7 x 8 − 3

.... (1)

b)   (11+ 13) x −20

.... (1)

c)   2 x 13²

.... (1)

d)   −13 − −27

.... (1)

End of paper 10

Answers

Paper 1
1) 172
2) 0.037
3) 29
4) 13
5) 64cm³
6) Many answers possible eg 1/3
7) £1.36
8) 4.12
9) 40 ° anticlockwise
10) 26
11) 3/7 43.7% 0.46 9/16
12) £265
13) -7y -1
14) 16/3 (5 ⅓)
15) 15%
16) 9/40
17) 8
18) 35%
19) 6 boxes
20) 140
21) 120g
22) 568.75 cm³

Paper 2
1) 3
2) 385/24 (16.04)
3) a) y →$\boxed{\times 5}$→$\boxed{+7}$→
   b) 72
4) 169
5) 61 degrees
6) one mark for each missing number

-4	**1**	0
3	-1	**-5**
-2	**-3**	2

7) 153.5cm
8) Morrisons (250g)
9) 7 dollars
10) £2500
11) a) 15km/hr
    b) 12km/hr
12) 5 athletes
13) 160
14) £100
15) a) 6/75 (0.08)
    b) 1/30 (0.03)
    c) 21/150 (0.14)
16) 14 blue, 26 red
17) 56

Paper 3
1) 813.35
2) 42
3) 17.55
4) 0.76
5) 16.76
6) 463
7) a) 25   b) 55
8) a) 60° b) 150° c) 105° d) 75°
9) a) y=11 b) y=3
10) 60cm
11) a) £12 b) £303 c) £125.50 d) 4
12) 7
13) 31/50 b) £150
14) a) 4% b) 5 days
15) 20 litres
16) 10%

Paper 4
1) 6576
2) 343
3) 1201
4) 65
5) $^{13}/_{24}$
6) $^{-11}/_{36}$
7) 39
8) $^{17}/_{40}$
9) 1.705m or 170.5cm or 1705mm
10) a) 384cm² b) 96cm c) 512cm²
11) £14.90
12) Coffee £1.20; Crème egg 35p
13) 25
14) £6.36
15) 3
16) 20km/hr
17) a) 54 mins
    b) 54 mins
    c) 9.28pm
    d) 12.04am
18) 117.5cm
19) 119cm
20) 180

Paper 5	Paper 6	Paper 7	Paper 8
1) 9.16	1) 5765g or 5.765kg	1) 500	1) 70
2) 80,000	2) 1.53	2) 6	2) 348
3) Many possible answers eg 10, 17, 24... ie. (7n+3)	3) 175	3) 8	3) 37
	4) 10.44	4) 3.25	4) 92.6
	5) 6570ml	5) 3	5) 16.34
4) 52	6) 6	6) -20	6) 410,509
5) 475	7) a) £2.70 b) £14.30	7) 5/6 > 0.4	7) 8
6) 79.2%	8) 3.0 bottles of milk	3/7 < 65%	8) 135°
7) a) 10 13 b) 157	9) a) 1.50am	37mm > 3cm	9) 36 mins
8) 366 boys 488 girls	b) 5.25pm	6.4m > 100cm	10) a) 60cm²
9) £42.90	10) 8 days	27/45 > 38%	b) 104 cm²
10) a) 5.10am	11) 144cm²	14/42 < 0.35	11) 26°
b) 12:05pm	12) 320cm²	8) 3	12) 336 boys and 288 girls
c) 13:35pm	13) 48 tiles	9) 39 sweets	13) 750g
11) 30cm²	14) a) 190	10) 49.5cm	14) £7.20
12) 81.8°	b) 6	11) a) -105 b) 126	15) 20%
13) 15	15) a) 600 b) i)120°	c) -150 d) 22	16) 50
14) Five 50p two 20p and three 10p	ii) 36° iii) 60°	e) 500 f) 45	17) a) 4n -13
15) 19	iv) 96° v) 48°	12) a) 0.5km b) 22.5km	b) 35 87 399
16) £15.29	16) £55.05	c) 12km	18) 135°
17) 250g tin is the best value	17) Otto is 25 and Harry is 27	13) 100	19) a) i)1/4 ii)5/24
18) a) 21 -6n	18) a) 24 b) 9	14) 2	b) i) 36° ii)75°
b) -39 -129 -459		15) 97°	c) i) 1/6 ii) 5/18
19) cone tetrahedron		16) 78	
		17) 42	

Paper 9
1) 3.333
2) 789
3) 7
4) 145,600
5) 7,200
6) 6.53L
7)

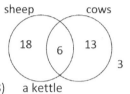

sheep   cows
18   6   13
                3

8) a kettle
9) x-10
10) 25cm
11) 351
12) 5
13) £175.50
14) 72cm^3
15) 67.79
16) £59.40
17) 0.245m^2
18) a) 25/4 b) 5/2
19) 40
20) 9/40
21) 17 boxes
22) 35/108

Paper 10
1) 14 15 16 17
2) 7.5
3) a) 107 b) 82 c) 10.7
   d) 877400 e) 87.74
4) a) Squared then
   times 4
   b) add 11 then
   times by 12
5) 2/3 > 60%
   0.810 < 0.810
   9^2 > 9 x 2
   5^3 < 127
6) 7.5 hrs
7) one mark for each
   correct row

Type	No.	angle
Sci fi	48	72
comedy	36	54
drama		
romance	60	90
action	84	126

8) 16m
9) -0.00006
10) 253691
11) a) 8/15   b) 1/6
    c) 3/10
12) 22
13) 4
14) a) 62   b) -480
    c) 338 d) 14

Printed in Great Britain
by Amazon

44962079R00037